DC
COMICS™

SUPERMAN™
SCIENCE

SEEING THROUGH WALLS

SUPERMAN™ AND THE SCIENCE OF SIGHT

BY AGNIESZKA BISKUP

SUPERMAN CREATED BY
JERRY SIEGEL
AND **JOE SHUSTER**
BY SPECIAL ARRANGEMENT
WITH THE JERRY SIEGEL FAMILY

CAPSTONE PRESS
a capstone imprint

Published by Capstone Press in 2016
A Capstone Imprint
1710 Roe Crest Drive
North Mankato, Minnesota 56003
www.mycapstone.com

Library of Congress Cataloging-in-Publication Data
Names: Biskup, Agnieszka, author.
Title: Seeing through walls : Superman and the science of sight / by Agnieszka Biskup.
Description: North Mankato, Minnesota : Capstone Press, 2016. | 2016 | Series: DC super
   heroes. Superman science | Audience: Ages 9–12. | Audience: Grade 3 to grade 6. |
   Includes bibliographical references and index.
Identifiers: LCCN 2016002664| ISBN 9781515709121 (library binding) | ISBN 9781515709169
   (paperback) | ISBN 9781515709206 (ebook pdf)
Subjects: LCSH: Vision—Juvenile literature. | Eye—Juvenile literature. | Superman
   (Fictitious character)—Juvenile literature.
Classification: LCC QP475.7 .B57 2016 | DDC 612.8/4—dc23
LC record available at http://lccn.loc.gov/2016002664

Summary: Explores the real-world science and engineering related to Superman's
super-vision.

Editorial Credits
Editor: Christopher Harbo
Designer: Bob Lentz
Production Specialist: Tori Abraham
Media Researcher: Eric Gohl

Photo Credits
iStockphoto: Peter Burnett, 16 (top), ShaneKato, 19 (bottom); Shutterstock: aeiddam, 23
(bottom), AkeSak, 15 (middle right), Antonio Gravante, 29, Carolina K. Smith MD, 15 (top
right), cbpix, 23 (top), CWA Studios, 27 (top), D. Kucharski K. Kucharska, 15 (top left), Dario
Sabljak, 15 (middle left), 24 (right), Dennis W. Donohue, 20, Designua, 6, 11, Donjiy, 21,
Evgeny Karandaev, 21 (background), Guido Akster, 22, holbox, 17 (bottom), Image Point
Fr, 24 (left), 28, itsmejust, 26 (front), 27 (bottom), Kovaleva_Ka, 10, lafayette-picture, 15
(bottom), Maximus256, 17 (top), Mmaxer, 7, OZMedia, 26 (back), pan demin, 19 (top),
Peter Hermes Furian, 8, 12, 13 (top), possohh, 25, Robert Przybysz, 13 (bottom), Sergey
Nivens, cover, snapgalleria, 9, Starover Sibiriak, 18, valeriiaarnaud, 16 (bottom),
wavebreakmedia, 14

Printed in the United States of America in North Mankato, Minnesota.
009667F16

TABLE OF CONTENTS

POWERFUL PEEPERS

Superman may be the most famous super hero of all time. Who doesn't know his origin story? Sent to Earth as a baby from the dying planet Krypton. Raised in Kansas as an ordinary human by Jonathan and Martha Kent. But he isn't ordinary, is he? As an alien from another planet, Superman has all sorts of powers that we can only dream about. Superman is not only fast and strong (he's not called the Man of Steel for nothing), but he also flies, is incredibly smart, and has super-vision. In fact, his eyes can emit **X-rays**, heat rays, and see at telescopic and microscopic levels.

As ordinary humans, we can't shoot heat beams out of our eyes. Although we only use our eyes to see, Superman's power is a reminder that the science behind vision is pretty extraordinary. And human sight is just the start. From vision enhancement to amazing animal eyes, there's more to sight than—well—meets the eye!

X-ray—an invisible high-energy beam of light that can pass through solid objects

FACT:

Superman's super-vision developed gradually from his 1938 appearance in comics. He first used X-ray vision in 1939, microscopic vision in 1940, and heat vision in 1949.

HUMAN SIGHT

The first time the people of Metropolis saw a blue blur zipping across the sky, they were stunned to see a man in flight. But they may not have stopped to think about something equally as amazing: their ability to see Superman in the first place. Take a peek at the science that makes sight possible.

LIGHT AND SIGHT

Understanding the science of sight begins with light. Just as Superman did as a baby, sunlight travels through space to reach our planet. But it doesn't travel on a rocket ship. It travels in energy waves. The full range of energy waves from the Sun is called the electromagnetic spectrum.

THE ELECTROMAGNETIC SPECTRUM

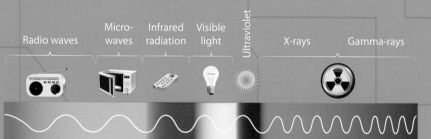

Radio waves | Micro-waves | Infrared radiation | Visible light | Ultraviolet | X-rays | Gamma-rays

Electromagnetic waves can be long, short, or somewhere in between. Most of these waves are invisible. We can't see shorter, higher energy waves such as gamma rays, X-rays, and **ultraviolet light**. We also can't see longer, lower energy **infrared light** waves, microwaves, and radio waves. Visible light, which is in the middle of the spectrum, is the only light energy we can see.

We call visible light from the Sun white light. But it's not just one color. It is actually made up different colors mixed together. The different colors in white light each have a different energy level. Have you learned the name "Roy G. Biv" to remember the colors of the rainbow? It stands for red, orange, yellow, green, blue, indigo, and violet. These colors are always in the same order because they are organized by their energy level. Red light has lower energy than green light. And violet light has the highest energy of all visible light.

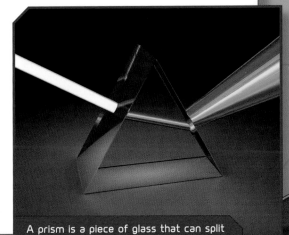

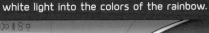
A prism is a piece of glass that can split white light into the colors of the rainbow.

ultraviolet light—an invisible form of light that can cause sunburns

infrared light—an invisible form of light that gives off heat

HUMAN VISION

Vision depends on your eyes' ability to detect light energy. How do they do it? **Reflected** light and the parts of your eyes are the keys.

Light reflects off everything around you. When you look at something, such as a tree, you see it because light bounces off it and into your eye. This light passes through your pupil and lens. It then makes an upside down and backward image of the tree on the retina at the back of the eye.

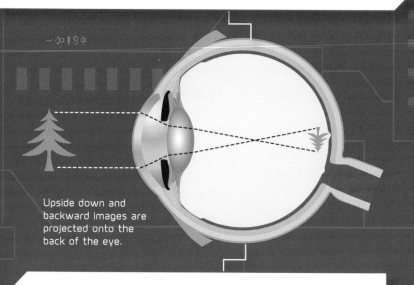

Upside down and backward images are projected onto the back of the eye.

The retina has cells called rods and cones that are **sensitive** to light. Rods are most sensitive to light and dark changes. They help you see at low light levels. Cones are active at higher light levels. They allow you to see color. The rods and cones change the image into an electrical signal. That signal zips through the optic nerve and directly to your brain. Your brain tells you what you see.

PARTS OF THE HUMAN EYE

IRIS
Uses a ring of muscle fibers to open and close the pupil.

PUPIL
Changes size to let more or less light into the eye.

CORNEA
Bends light into the eye and protects the eye from wind and dust.

OPTIC NERVE
Carries messages from the retina to the brain.

RETINA
Contains light-sensitive rods and cones, which change light into an electrical signal that the brain understands.

LENS
Changes shape to focus light onto the retina.

reflect—to bounce off an object

sensitive—able to detect or react to the slightest change in something

SEEING COLOR

Superman's eyes can see through walls and shoot beams to cut through steel. Although we can only wish for these powers, our eyes do have the amazing ability to see a remarkable range of colors. In fact, most people can see about one million colors. How? It's a tag-team combo of reflected light and the cones in our eyes.

The color of an object depends on the **wavelengths** of light it reflects and **absorbs**. For instance, a ripe banana looks yellow because it absorbs every color wavelength except yellow. The yellow wavelengths are reflected. Likewise, an apple looks red because it absorbs every color wavelength except red.

But reflecting and absorbing colors is only half of the story. Each of your eyes has about six million cone cells in its retina. And each one of those cones is most sensitive to red, green, or blue. When you see a banana, the reflected light stimulates the cones in the retina to different degrees. A signal then travels along the optic nerve to your brain. Your brain processes the signal and tells you that you're seeing yellow.

CONES AND ROOS OF THE RETINA

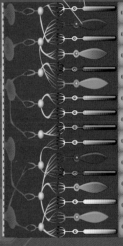

Cone cell   Rod cell

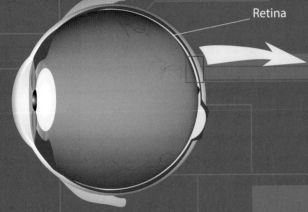

Retina

COLOR BLINDNESS

Some people have cone cells that lack certain color-sensitive pigments. This condition causes color blindness. About 1 in 12 men and 1 in 200 women are red-green color blind. That means they can't easily tell the difference between red and green. In very rare cases, people can also be blue-yellow color blind. And absolutely color-blind people are the most rare. They only see the world in shades of gray.

wavelength—the distance between two peaks of a wave

absorb—to soak up

pigment—a substance that gives something a particular color when it is present in it or is added to it

ENHANCING SIGHT

Clark Kent may wear glasses, but he certainly doesn't need them to see. They are part of his clever disguise as a mild-mannered reporter. For the rest of us, glasses, as well as microscopes and telescopes, actually improve our vision.

CORRECTIVE LENSES

People need glasses when the lenses in their eyes don't curve correctly to focus clearly on an object. For some people, an incorrect curve causes nearsightedness. They can see things up close, but objects in the distance look blurry. For others, a different incorrect curve causes farsightedness. They can see faraway objects, but close ones are blurry.

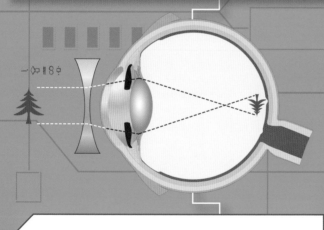

Glasses have custom-made lenses that bend light to help focus it on the retina. **Concave** lenses help nearsighted people see faraway objects. These lenses are thinner in the middle than around the edges. Light passing through these lenses bends outward.

Farsighted people use **convex** lenses to help them see up-close objects. Convex lenses are thin at the edges but thick in the middle. They bend light inward.

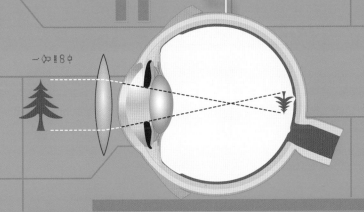

LASER SURGERY

Glasses aren't the only option for correcting vision. For a more permanent solution, some people choose laser eye surgery. Surgeons use lasers to carefully reshape and correct the corneas. Once they're repaired, no additional lenses are needed in front of the eyes to correct vision.

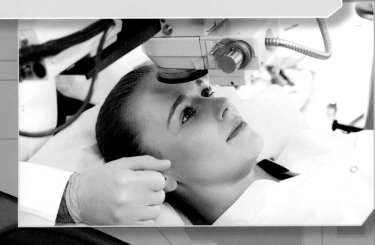

concave—hollow and curved, like the inside of a bowl
convex—curved outward, like the outside of a ball

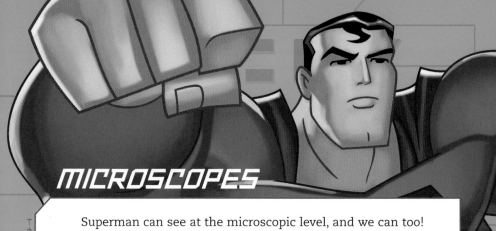

MICROSCOPES

Superman can see at the microscopic level, and we can too! But because we weren't born on Krypton, we need microscopes to do it. Visit any lab in the world and you'll likely find a **compound** microscope. Like eyeglasses, these microscopes use lenses to bend light. Instead of just bringing objects into focus, these lenses make objects look hundreds of times larger.

Binocular compound microscopes have two eyepieces instead of one.

Compound microscopes **magnify** objects by using at least two lenses. The lens closest to your eye is called the eyepiece. The lens nearest the object you are looking at is called the objective lens. The objective lens magnifies an object first. Then the eyepiece magnifies the image from the objective lens a second time.

Microscopes allow us to explore a world that is normally too small to see. Scientists use them to study plant cells, insect wings, and other tiny living and nonliving things. Doctors use microscopes to study blood and tissue samples. And companies that create tiny objects—such as computer chips—use microscopes to inspect their products.

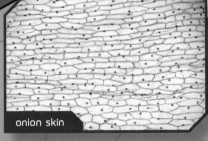
onion skin

louse

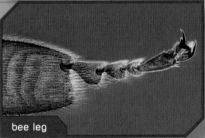
bee leg

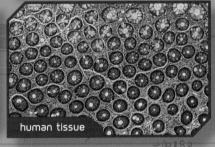
human tissue

ELECTRON MICROSCOPES

Electron microscopes are the most powerful microscopes on the planet. Instead of rays of light, they use beams of electrons to create a very detailed image of the tiniest things. While compound microscopes magnify objects up to about 2,000 times, electron microscopes can magnify objects a million times or more! They allowed scientists to see viruses and atoms for the first time. And they can see everyday items—such as pollen grains or an ant's head—in amazing detail.

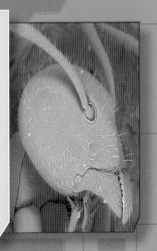

compound—having two or more parts

magnify—to make something look larger than it really is

electron—a tiny particle in an atom that travels around the nucleus

TELESCOPES

Superman has the eyes of a hawk. He can focus his sight to see objects clearly from miles away. For mere mortals like ourselves, the tool we use to see great distances is a telescope. Most telescopes are either **refracting** or reflecting telescopes.

Like microscopes, refracting telescopes use an objective lens and an eyepiece. But instead of making small objects look bigger, these lenses make distant objects look closer. To do this, the objective lens collects light from a distant object. Then the eyepiece magnifies it to make it look closer. The bigger the objective lens, the brighter the image and the more it can be magnified.

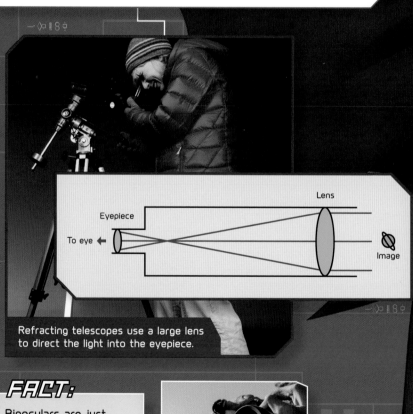

Refracting telescopes use a large lens to direct the light into the eyepiece.

FACT:

Binoculars are just two small telescopes attached to each other, one for each eye.

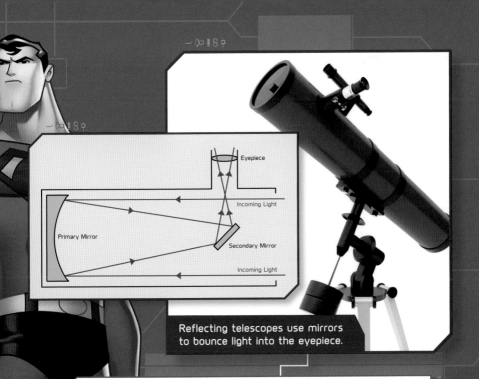

Reflecting telescopes use mirrors to bounce light into the eyepiece.

Reflecting telescopes work similarly to refracting telescopes. But instead of an objective lens, they use a primary mirror to gather light. This curved mirror reflects the light toward the secondary mirror. This mirror then reflects the light to the eyepiece. The eyepiece magnifies the object to make it look closer.

GREAT CANARY TELESCOPE

The Great Canary Telescope is the world's largest telescope and, like most big telescopes, a reflector. It sits on a mountaintop in the Canary Islands off the northwest coast of Africa. Its mirror spans 34.1 feet (10.4 meters) across.

refract—to bend light as it passes through a substance at an angle

ANIMAL VISION

Considering Superman is an alien from another planet, it's not totally surprising that his vision is so different from ours. What may be surprising is the number of creatures on Earth whose eyes seem just as alien as his!

NO EYES, MANY EYES

When it comes to animal sight, eyeballs aren't the only option. Many animals have compound eyes. These eyes are made up of hundreds of separate units. The more units, the better the animal can see. An ant's eye has several hundred units. A housefly has a few thousand. And dragonflies can have 30,000 units in each eye. Compound eyes are excellent at detecting motion. That's one of the reasons it can be difficult to swat a fly. It spots your hand moving toward it. But compound eyes aren't so good at seeing fine details.

COMPOUND EYES

dragonfly

Other animals don't have eyes in the traditional sense at all. Earthworms have hundreds of little light-sensitive cells called eyespots around their heads and tails. These cells help them find the cool, dark places they like to go. Leeches, caterpillars, and jellyfish have eyespots too. And sea stars can have an eyespot on each arm. Depending on the species, a sea star can have up to 40 eyes! But even with all those eyes, they don't see much. They mostly detect the direction of light and large shadows.

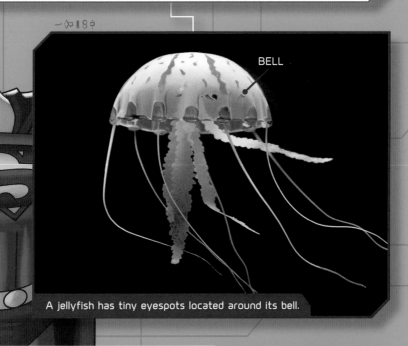

BELL

A jellyfish has tiny eyespots located around its bell.

SCALLOPS

Scallops probably win as the most-eyed creatures on Earth. A single scallop may have more than 100 eyes! Each of these eyes, located all around its mantle, has a lens and retina. They work together to alert the animal of changes in light and motion. The scallop can see very rough images—enough to warn it against predators.

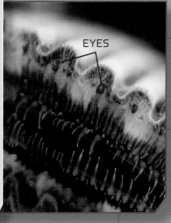

EYES

EAGLE-EYED

Although our eyesight isn't as sharp as Superman's, some animals have incredibly keen peepers. The term "eagle-eyed" exists for good reason—eagles have very sharp eyesight! They can see four to five times farther than the average person. If you swapped eyes with an eagle, you could stand on top of a 10-story building and see an ant crawling on the ground. You could even spot a rabbit from more than 1 mile (1.6 kilometer) away. Now that's super hero-level eyesight!

Bald eagles use their keen eyesight to swoop down and snatch fish right out of the water.

Eagles see so well because their eyes are huge. Although the average eagle only weighs about 10 pounds (4.5 kilograms), its eyes can be as large as a grown man's. Bigger eyes mean better vision because they let in more light. And the larger the eye, the larger the image projected on the retina.

Larger eyes see finer details, much like a large TV screen shows more details than a small tablet screen.

Imagine watching a movie on a tablet versus a big-screen TV. You can see many more details on the larger screen. Eagle retinas are also more densely coated with cones than ours. They allow the birds to see much more clearly than we do. In addition, eagles have excellent color vision and can see ultraviolet light too.

NIGHT VISION

The power to see through the darkest night isn't just for super heroes. Some animals have night vision too. Nocturnal animals are most active at night. To help them see, their huge eyes have wider pupils, larger lenses, and larger retinas. These features allow their eyes to collect more light in dark conditions. For example, owls have eyes that fill more than one half of their skulls. Their forward-facing eyes are so big they can't move them. To make up for their fixed eyes, they can swivel their heads 270 degrees. This ability gives them a wide field of view.

Owls use their huge eyes to hunt at night.

The *tapetum lucidum* in a shark's eye glows when it reflects light.

Some animals have reflectors, called the *tapetum lucidum*, in the backs of their eyes. These reflectors can double the amount of light their eyes can use. Have you ever seen a cat at night with glowing eyes? What you're seeing is the tapetum reflecting light. Other animals with tapetums include raccoons, cows, sharks, crocodiles, deer, zebras, lions, and moths.

FIELD OF VIEW

How much an animal can see without turning its head is called its field of view. Predators, such as lions, wolves, and owls, have eyes that face forward. Their eyes give them good **depth perception**, which helps them find and catch prey. Prey animals, such as deer, zebras, and chickens, have eyes that face sideways. Their depth perception is not too good. But their side-facing eyes give them a large field of vision. They can see almost all the way around their bodies, usually giving them time to see and flee predators.

depth perception—the ability to judge the distance of objects and the space between them at different distances

BEYOND ORDINARY SIGHT

It's no secret that Superman can melt icebergs using heat vision and see through concrete walls using X-ray vision. But did you know humans also have their own versions of heat and X-ray vision? Check out what we can see with a little help from technology.

HEAT VISION

Superman, cats, and owls have no problem seeing in dimly lit areas. But people need a little help. Luckily, technology can bring things to light.

One method for seeing in dark places depends on heat. **Thermal** imaging equipment detects infrared light waves. These invisible waves carry heat. All objects give off some amount of infrared waves. Thermal cameras change these invisible waves into light you can see. They can detect people, animals, and objects by the heat patterns they emit.

40.3 °C

20.3

Thermal cameras detect heat given off by everything, including us.

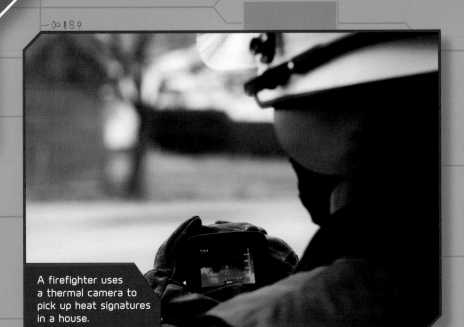

A firefighter uses a thermal camera to pick up heat signatures in a house.

Thermal imaging can be used at night for seeing in the dark. It is also used during the day to see things through smoke, heavy fog, and dust storms. Firefighters use thermal imaging to help find people in smoke-filled buildings. Thermal imaging equipment is also used by the military and police for security purposes. It can reveal whether an area has been recently disturbed, such as when something is buried in the ground. Law enforcement has used thermal imaging to find hidden drugs, money, and bodies.

thermal—having to do with heat or holding in heat

X-RAY VISION

When it comes to his eyes, Superman's most famous power is his X-ray vision. In comic books and movies, this superpower allows him to peer through walls as if they were invisible. In real life, X-rays work a little differently.

X-rays are a high-energy form of electromagnetic **radiation** that we can't see. These rays have so much energy they can travel through things that ordinary, visible light can't. X-rays are often used in medicine to diagnose and treat illnesses.

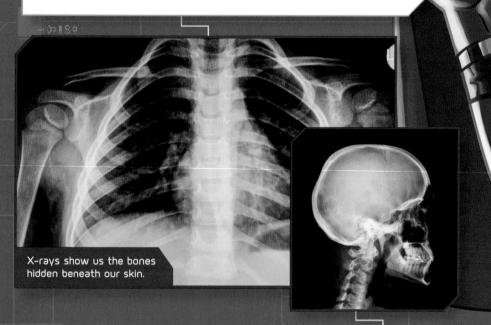

X-rays show us the bones hidden beneath our skin.

Medical X-rays are made by placing the part of the body to be examined between a beam of X-rays and a plate containing film. Hard materials like bones absorb X-rays very well. Soft tissues, such as skin and muscle, allow the rays to pass right through. The X-rays that pass through the body strike the photographic plate. Dense bones show up as white and softer tissues look gray.

FACT:

The ability of X-rays to damage living tissue can be used for good. X-rays are used to kill cancer cells in radiation therapy treatment.

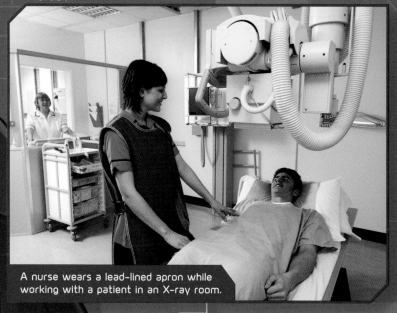

A nurse wears a lead-lined apron while working with a patient in an X-ray room.

As X-rays pass through the body, they can damage living tissue because they are so energetic. For this reason, lead-lined aprons are often placed over body parts we don't want X-rays to pass through. Lead blocks X-rays because it is so dense. Interestingly, lead is the one material Superman's X-ray vision can't see through either.

WILHELM ROENTGEN

German physicist Wilhelm Roentgen discovered X-rays in 1895. He called them "X" rays because he didn't know what they were. The very first image taken using X-rays was of his wife's hand. When she saw the picture of the bones beneath her skin, she exclaimed, "I have seen my death." Roentgen won the first Nobel Prize in Physics in 1901 for his discovery.

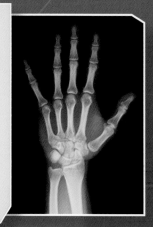

radiation—rays of energy given off by certain elements

THE FUTURE OF SIGHT

Superman-like sight may be in our future. Scientists and engineers are developing all sorts of exciting technologies to enhance our vision. In fact, a telescopic contact lens has already been invented. It allows people to zoom in their vision almost three times. It was created to help people with age-related macular degeneration (AMD). This condition makes it difficult to see fine details, such as type on a page. Telescopic contacts allow people with AMD to zoom in on these details.

A woman takes an eye test to detect AMD.

Researchers at the University of Michigan have also developed a super-thin infrared light sensor that could be layered onto contact lenses. This sensor could one day be used to allow people to see in the dark. Instead of wearing bulky night-vision goggles, soldiers would simply pop in a pair of contacts.

bionic—relating to mechanical replacement body parts
implant—a device inserted into the body by surgery

High-tech contact lenses and bionic eyes may be the future of superhuman sight.

A **bionic** eye has also been developed for the legally blind. The Argus II Retinal Prosthesis System uses a tiny camera in a patient's glasses to capture images. The images change into electrical pulses that are sent to an **implant** in the retina. The implant sends the pulses through the optic nerve to the brain. The brain makes sense of the images and creates patterns of light. Although the Argus II doesn't restore normal vision, it does allow people to sense objects and even see some color.

CONCLUSION

For the Man of Steel, powerful eyesight is just one tool for battling the forces of evil. For the rest of us, his eyes are a reminder of the incredible science behind vision. From the way our eyes use light to technology that enhances eyesight, the science behind sight is endless.

GLOSSARY

absorb (ab-ZORB)—to soak up

bionic (bye-ON-ik)—relating to mechanical replacement body parts

compound (KAHM-paund)—having two or more parts

concave (kahn-KAYV)—hollow and curved, like the inside of a bowl

convex (kahn-VEKS)—curved outward, like the outside of a ball

depth perception (DEPTH pur-SEP-shuhn)—the ability to judge the distance of objects and the space between them at different distances

electron (i-LEK-tron)—a tiny particle in an atom that travels around the nucleus

implant (IM-plant)—a device inserted into the body by surgery

infrared light (IN-fruh-red LITE)—an invisible form of light that gives off heat

magnify (MAG-nih-fye)—to make something look larger than it really is

pigment (PIG-muhnt)—a substance that gives something a particular color when it is present in it or is added to it

radiation (ray-dee-AY-shuhn)—rays of energy given off by certain elements

reflect (ri-FLEKT)—to bounce off an object

refract (ri-FRACT)—to bend light as it passes through a substance at an angle

sensitive (SEN-suh-tive)—able to detect or react to the slightest change in something

thermal (THUR-muhl)—having to do with heat or holding in heat

ultraviolet light (uhl-truh-VYE-uh-lit LITE)—an invisible form of light that can cause sunburns

wavelength (WAYV-length)—the distance between two peaks of a wave

X-ray (EKS-ray)—an invisible high-energy beam of light that can pass through solid objects

READ MORE

Clark, John O. E. *The Basics of Light.* Core Concepts. New York: Rosen Publishing, 2015.

Huddle, Rusty, and Jennifer Viegas. *The Eye in 3D.* The Human Body in 3D. New York: Rosen Publishing, 2016.

Kukla, Lauren. *Light at Work.* Science at Work. Minneapolis: Abdo Publishing, 2017.

Sheen, Barbara. *Artificial Eyes.* Tech Bytes. Chicago: Norwood House Press, 2016.

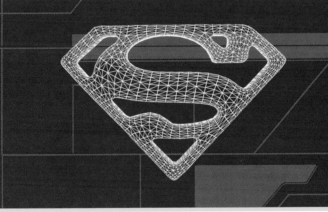

INTERNET SITES

FactHound offers a safe, fun way to find Internet sites related to this book. All of the sites on FactHound have been researched by our staff.

Here's all you do:

Visit *www.facthound.com*

Type in this code: 9781515709121

INDEX